Alec's Legacy

Alec's Legacy

Frank Robinson

Published by ALR LLC
3420 Pump Road, #200
Richmond, VA 23233-1111

ISBN 0-9788504-0-8

First Printing 2006

For permissions please see page 127, in the section entitled
"Notes."

For more information and to order copies of *Alec's Legacy*,
please visit our website, **www.alecslegacy.com**

Cover design: Kyle G. Hunter
Text design: Wendy Holdman
Interior art: Carol Wolf

Printed in the United States of America at BookMobile,
Minneapolis, Minnesota.

Contents

Part I   Diary Excerpts

Part II   Miracles

Part III—The Community

Dedication

To our family, who have stood with us and loved us through our darkest days.

To Sandy, who was our strength.

To Sharon and Doug, Lourie and Ken, Margaret and Jerry, who were our comfort.

To Reese, who was our rock.

To Bev and Ted, for their faithfulness.

To Andrew, Blake, Chris, Eliza, Erica, Hayden, Jayson, Johnny, Kristin, Lauren, Logan, Ryan, Tim, Whitney and Zach, who loved him, too.

To our friends, who have sustained us with immeasurable caring.

To Ray and Darrel, who never let the light go out.

To the Stettinius Fund of the Community Foundation of Greater Richmond, for the rare opportunity to compose these writings.

Part I

Diary Excerpts

Purpose

This book is written for those who mourn their children.

And, for those in the greater community who co-mourn, whether they are grandparents, family friends or peers of the lost child.

It is written to provide a voice to a parent's pain and feelings—as honestly and openly as it can. It may reflect only our family's experience, but it is an attempt to provide some articulation of what it feels like to lose a child, and in doing so, to allow others who must walk this lonely road to know others have traversed this path before them.

It is intended to also serve as a guide to family and community in supporting a family in mourning—skills which we are not well taught.

It is intended to give voice to experiences which are difficult to explain and challenging to discuss for many.

It is a meager attempt at expressing gratitude to a family and community who have provided extraordinary generosity in their caring and love.

When we lost our son, we were devastated and overcome with grief. We searched desperately for comfort and guidance, particularly in the printed word. So much of what we read seemed sanitized and clinical. None of it reflected the anguish I felt as a father, spoken from the first person.

I did not want to be patronized. I did not want palliative religious tracts. I did not care about the five stages of grief. And, while I found some comfort in church, I felt I was in the house of a God who had deceived me.

I wanted to know if others felt this excruciating pain, this absolute sense of abandonment, this violation, this cruel farce of life. I wanted to know if every grieving parent felt he or she could go crazy at any minute, and that virtually everything he or she had achieved and worked for was meaningless. I wanted some resonance for my rage. I wanted to know if others felt so cheated by life and by God. I wanted to know if the cacophony of noise and emotion in my mind was normal, and if it would it ever go away. I wanted to know honestly how others experienced such depth and breadth of grief.

Ultimately, there were two works in which I found solace. The classic, *A Grief Observed*, by C.S. Lewis, records his grief after the death of his wife. *Lament for a Son*, by Nicholas Wolterstorff, is a poetic and moving series of personal writings reflecting the loss of his son Eric. Both books present the agony and journey of grief in very personal and profound description. Both books let me know I was not alone.

I share our experiences after the loss of our son, Alec, to provide, hopefully, another anchor to parents who grieve. Each of our grief experiences is unique—there is importance in knowing that—but there is commonality as well. I kept wanting to find something that told me, "Yes, he knows."

These thoughts and expressions are from my diaries in the first two years after losing Alec. They are momentary snapshots of feelings and insights as we moved through this very challenging time in our lives. In this experience of loss there is no standard against which to measure. It is all quicksand. It is my hope that sharing provides some solid ground.

The inclusions here are not in chronological order. Grieving is not some predictable incline that one gradually mounts. It is more like climbing a rock pile, where you slip back and begin again all the more bruised.

And, with intention, there is no resolution in these writings. Yes, there is progress and change, but it would be dishonest to say it is done.

In truth, we all mourn alone—in our own way, with our own thoughts and on our own schedules. It is a singularly difficult experience. If this book provides any comfort to another person in pain, it has achieved its purpose.

Where does the life of a child go?

Where does the life of a child go when he dies?

We step on an ant, or swat a fly, and we assume it is just gone.

But a child? With all of that energy, curiosity, potential and love? Where does the life of a child go?

To think it dissipates into thin air is too hideous to consider.

Shattered

On June 3, 2003, my 19-year-old son took an evening ride down a country road that he loved and had driven a hundred times. He was on his way to meet friends to go to a movie.

For some unknowable reason—a deer, a turkey, a momentary flash of sunset light—his car veered off the road, traveling under 35 miles per hour. He went through a wooden livestock fence. Somehow, all the elements of the universe aligned, and one of the boards penetrated the driver's side window, hitting him in the neck, killing him almost instantly.

My life changed forever.

Eventually, a friend asked how it felt.

"Shattered," I answered.

Like a laminated windshield hit by a rock, somehow I am still held together, but my world, my life, my understanding of reality are utterly and completely shattered into tiny little disconnected pieces.

God Letter 1

My God, how could you let this happen?

My son is dead?

My wife called me with a voice I have never heard. I am away—too far away.

My son needs me. My family needs me. I am alone and desolate.

I sit in this airport with no planes, no cars, no buses. It is 3:30 A.M.

They do not care that my son is dead, nor that my life is crumbling before me.

This must be a nightmare that will go away in the morning.

I am cold, and I am utterly alone.

Lament

This was not supposed to happen to me. I have loved this boy since he was born. It was me he first smiled at. I have fathered him, and held him, and guided him and loved him as purely and totally as I have known how.

This was not supposed to happen to his mother. She adored him from the moment he was conceived. She nursed him, and carried him. She worried after him, and gently led him year by year. She doted on him, and celebrated his every achievement.

This was not supposed to happen to his brother. The little brother he looked after, whose every like and dislike he knew at age 5. Who looked up to him. Whom he admired with a sense of wonder. The brothers who teased and aggravated, and who had grown into such fine young men. His brother who should not have to know this loss so young. Who will know his loss through every year of his life ahead.

This was not supposed to happen to his grandparents. They are nearly 80, and have lived good lives. They have worked hard, sacrificed for their families. They have loved these boys beyond measure—the pride of their old age. Why now should they suffer such pain? Why is this a part of their lives in these late days?

This was not supposed to happen to his friends—those who were drawn to him for his kindness and friendship. Those who sparked his smile which in turn warmed their hearts. Those who shared his sense of fun.

Those he watched over, worried about and reassured. They are too young to have lost their innocence.

This was not supposed to happen to his aunts and uncles and cousins—this extended family which has always meant so much to us. This was not supposed to happen to our friends, who now work to hold together our shattered lives and make sense out of their own.

This was not supposed to happen to him—this kind and gentle young man, who had so much joy and zest for life. This young man who had so much potential to do good and give back to this world. This young man who would have lived his life so well. He was faithful to You in his beliefs. He lived his life with integrity. He savored this world you created, and gave thanks for it.

Oh, God, why have you forsaken him?

Why have you forsaken us all?

Alec Letter 4

My Dear Alec,

Where are you, my son? I see you everywhere and I find you nowhere. I cannot remember when you were not a palpable part of my life.

I still feel you and expect to catch a glimpse of you. It seems impossible that you won't be calling or coming home for the weekend.

Last week Reese said "we don't want you dead and we miss you."

It angered me that he said it out loud—that you were dead. After all these weeks, it still sounds so horrible.

I don't want you dead. I am not willing to give you up so easily—no matter what the evidence. It is going to take a long, long time to give you up. Probably never. Really, never. You are too much a part of me.

This is a battle I know I can only lose, but I still want to fight.

God Letter 3

My God,

Is this how you felt when Jesus was crucified?

Can even God know such anguish?

Christ was resurrected in three days.

How long will I have to wait for my son?

The Veil

I live behind a veil, now.

It is darker here. Colder.

Is it possible no-one sees it? Does it make me invisible?

How can they rush about, pushing past me in the store?

Does no-one care that he is dead?

One day we will all be dead.

How foolishly our lives are spent.

The veil clarifies. It filters the significant from the non-significant.

What endures but our love?

Truth of God

My Dear Friend,

One of the more meaningful things I have read in a long time:

> "When your mind asks 'Why?' you realize how easily it is satisfied with a superficial answer."
> "When your heart asks 'Why?' it wants nothing but the truth of God."[1]

That is exactly what I want—the truth of God—nothing else! His truth seems so elusive in some ways, and so obvious in others. Every day I see the bounty, the beauty, the order, the interconnectedness, the complexity, the exuberance of this world—God's world.

I know it was created with love and generosity.

But when it comes to my son—this precious gift—a gift I always have known came from God, for he was too miraculous to come from anywhere else—where do I find God's truth?

Why did he die so young?

No one seems to have answers. God seems so hesitant to answer. I tell Him that I deserve an answer—this is too great a price to pay without an answer. He owes me at least this.

Where do I find the truth of God?

Friend Letter 2

My Dear Friend,

My life is a constant contradiction these days.

I have come to understand grief as a confusing rush of multiple emotions. "Normal" is to feel one emotion at a time. Grief is to have too many to manage—they overwhelm the nervous system—my body quakes.

When I feel any emotion it is matched by the exact opposite. When I feel joy, I also feel sadness. When I laugh, I feel a cry of pain. When I feel regret, I feel relief. There are no filters.

I go to work to find focus, and hate being there because it seems so trivial. When I stay at home I cannot sit still or rest—rest allows too much thought, which leads to too many unanswerable questions.

It is exhausting to mourn.

God Letter 5

My God,

A friend says you are big enough to absorb my anger. Is it true?

Dare I tell you how much I hate what Alec's death has done to us?

Dare I invoke your wrath?

If this is not punishment for some unknown sin, you could not have found a consequence more devastatingly punishing.

If this is random and arbitrary, we live in a world more cruel and cold than I expect you to have created.

If you are an all knowing and loving God, and this is part of some greater plan, then I want revelation. I want some knowledge of how losing Alec from this earth makes sense and makes the universe a better place.

"Seek and you shall find. Ask and it shall be given." I am asking, Lord. I await your answer.

Heart Grate

All loss is painful, but the loss of a child must be the most deeply felt pain of all.

It violates all of the assumptions one makes about the world—all of the things you unconsciously believe in and expect will happen. It vaporizes your trust. It snaps all of those emotional ties which began to knot at conception and grew and grew beyond one's imagination with each passing day.

". . . just when he'd think it couldn't get worse, think a body couldn't hold more hurt. . . . the loss an infinity inside him. Like how many times you can bisect a line. They call it heartbreak, but not Matley. Matley learned it was not that clean, nowhere near that quick, he learned it was a heartgrating, this forever loss in slow motion, forever loss without diminishment of loss, without recession, without ease, the grating."[2]

This is how it feels to lose a child. "Forever loss." "An infinity inside."

Alec Letter 2

My Dear Alec,

A few days ago Reese told me that we would survive this, but from now on I would "walk with a limp."

I intend to defy that. I don't think you would want me to walk with a limp for the rest of my life. I will honor you with my energy and my living. I may have a hole in my heart, but that is between you and me. You will always be missed, but I shall not limp. You never would, my love.

God Letter 2

My God, why this boy?

This boy with such promise.

This boy of endless smiles and zest for life. Smart and strong, handsome, fun, loved by so many.

Why this boy, God?

Why would you endow him with so many gifts and potential for doing such good in this world, and then take him so soon?

Surely, there are drug dealers and criminals you could have chosen. Those who will never contribute to our world.

Why the best? The kindest? The most beautiful?

Certainly you knew his gifts. So bright a star extinguished from this human constellation.

Why this boy?

Music

Since Alec died I cannot sing.

Wherever the capacity to sing resides within the human soul, it is too close to this hole, this emptiness, to allow such expression. Singing must be some fundamental capacity—something deep near the utter center of humanness.

Listening to music is difficult as well. The most difficult songs are songs of joy and praise. One has to be in a very different place to sing or listen to these. I think people who sing songs of praise do so in total innocence, or ignorance. I envy them their innocence.

I used to think love songs were about romantic love, but love is love. Love songs are just as much about my love for Alec as any other love I have known.

> "I love him.
> I'm his.
> And, everything he is,
> I am, too."[3]

Cemeteries

I never thought I would spend so much of my time, at this stage of my life, in a cemetery?

I find comfort here. I feel so much less alone.

As I look over the endless graves, I realize that every person buried here was loved, and has been mourned. A cemetery is like a great repository of love. The tomb stones reverberate with it.

They buried a part of me the day they buried Alec. Part of me lies in this ground. I will not be complete again, until I lay here as well.

Is this not where we are all headed? To a great repository of love?

Suicide

When one's life is shattered, there is a specter which lurks—something everyone thinks about but few are willing to discuss—suicide.

Have I thought about it? Of course. But, always with a sense that I would not act. When one's loss and pain become deep enough and persistent enough, this seems an understandable direction for the mind and heart to explore. What a relief it would be to spin off this earth and leave the gravity of this life.

But, I know the pain and suffering my family have endured, and I could never consider adding to this for them.

I have come to understand suicide in new ways. Mostly that it is about seeking relief, not creating more suffering. Death is an unfortunate side effect of ending the pain, not a goal in itself.

I have heard suicide described as a "permanent solution to a short-term problem," and a "coward's way out."

In response to the first, I can only say that my son's death does not feel like a "short-term problem." Nor will it ever. It will never be my "short-term problem."

To the second, it is wrong to mistake cowardliness with defeat. Someone who is pushed to the precipice of suicide has already fought many a difficult battle with the demons of grief. Grief can be an unrelenting foe, and I suspect those who are conquered by it are depleted, and in the lonely struggle, have lost their sense of connection to other people in the world. Inner pain is deafening and blinding—isolating—and one can lose his place in the world with alarming speed.

The problem with suicide is that it does not end your pain—it just passes it on to the ones who love you, with additional dimensions of sorrow.

One makes a difficult choice—to own the pain, or pass it on.

The House

Friends ask if we won't sell the house.

"Wouldn't it be easier?"

I see him in the yard mowing the grass, in the driveway working on his car, in the street zooming on his skateboard.

I see him in the school gym, at Friday night football games, on the soccer field, at the sporting goods store, at the hardware store looking at pocket knives.

I see him at the emergency room of the hospital getting yet another stitch.

I see him at the airport impatiently awaiting departure for his next trip.

I see him buying school supplies, at the music store poring over CD's, in the aisles of the supermarket as I pass his favorite foods, at the department store when I find the things I would buy him for Christmas, or his birthday, or just because.

I see him at the pizza place, at his favorite Vietnamese restaurant with his girlfriend, with every cup of hot-and-sour soup.

I see him at the car dealership pining over his dream car, in the audio department preparing to install oversized speakers in the old family Volvo station wagon, at the DMV getting his first license.

I see him at the Christmas tree lot.

The house is where we shared our lives, joined in meals, celebrated holidays, marked his height on the door frame as he grew, and buried his pet iguana.

His life was so much bigger than the house.

Would that it could be that easy.

Tidy Grief

Odd how people want to limit grief—control grief. After a week, after a year . . . all the assumed "shoulds" to make it short, make it fast, make it tidy. Like a handkerchief—if you fold and refold it, starch it and iron it flat, that its true dimension might disappear.

Grief is, in truth, multidimensional. Rooted in the present, it extends back into your past, and projects onto your future. It is emotional, mental, physical, and indeed metaphysical. Like a cancer it metastasizes through your life, showing up in places and times where it is never expected.

This is the crazy-making character of grief: today a crying binge; Tuesday, can't eat; Wednesday, diatribes with God; Thursday, exhaustion; Friday, insatiable appetite; Saturday, who will I be?

Yesterday I was a father? Today I am what? One child less of a father. A less father? We don't have a word for this.

Grief cannot be contained. It will be expressed in some way—even if you try to suppress it, or ignore it, or tidy it up. It will find its way out of your soul into your life. And into the lives of others.

Grief ultimately visits us all. Is this why people work so hard to push it along, and pack it away? "Keep it contained and maybe it won't reach me."

Like the stretching green cloud of the plague in the classic movie "The Ten Commandments" which kills the first-born sons of all Egyptians, it ultimately finds us.

For Mary Ann

You must change your expectations, my friend. I am not the person I used to be.

I now have my own B.C. and A.D. (Before the Crash; After he Died)

The chasm between is too great to cross back over.

My life has been re-directed in ways I cannot predict, nor could have imagined.

Had I lost a limb or been disfigured, I think you might find it easier to accept the "new" me—the me I am becoming. My disfigurement is invisible to most—some cannot see, others are too pained to look at such brokenness—the struggle to make sense of anything.

If you loved me before, please love me now. I need your love more than I ever did in the past. I need a hand to steady me, and an ear to listen to the chaos of my soul.

I know returning to the person "I was" would be more comfortable for you.

That person is, also, now gone.

Please walk beside me on this journey. I understand it is hard for you, dear one. It is hard for all of us.

I need your strength. I ask you to embrace me when I lose hope. Let us share who I have become. . . . who you have become. You, too, have been changed.

This road to eternity is obscured in fog, with many unsure footholds.

Walk with me.

We cannot go it alone.

Who speaks?
God? Father? Son?

"I am the one whose love

overcomes you, already with you

when you think to call my name. . . ."[4]

My Friend,

I am coming to the realization that I have to make peace with this. If I am to honor my son, I have to find a way to move forward—to live life fully and joyously, as he did.

Carpe Diem! That was his motto, and he lived it. That will be a challenge with a broken heart. But I know in my mind and in my heart the beauty of this world, its complexity, its wonders. These are not accidental.

And, if I know how incredible it is, and that life renews every day in unbelievable ways, and that we are an intrinsic part of these cycles, should I not find hope?

My mind knows this. My heart cannot yet accept that my Alec should part of this everlasting cycle so soon.

How does one align the heart and the mind with a loss so great?

Not yet. But someday.

Alec Letter 5

My Dear Alec,

We were at JMU yesterday for Parent's Weekend. I thought of you with every step—that you had walked those paths and entered those buildings full of life and joy. Where are you now?

It was not so much haunting as it was lonely. You should be there with all of those young people—with all of your friends. They, too, miss you. Your pictures are in all of their rooms. You have not disappeared from any of our lives. Our memories are precious.

I looked at all of those kids on campus, and I wondered, "Why you?" So many who assume so much in life, who take it for granted, who are reckless. Why you?

No-one looked as special as you, or as kind as you. No-one had your smile—nothing close. I wouldn't wish death on any of them, but if there is a place for them here, why not a place for you?

Friend Letter 1

My Friend,

I read today that grief is a gift. It is a consequence of having loved so much. To avoid grief, one would have to avoid love. And, not to have loved would mean to not have lived.

Would I have chosen not to love to avoid grief? Never. Love has filled my life. It has made it wonderful. I have been blessed with generous and deep love all of my life.

I love Alec with all of my heart and soul. No father could have loved a son more.

Now I pay the price.

Walter

I spoke with Walter the other evening about the contacts and coincidences we have experienced.

Walter is a scientist—very bright, highly trained. He understands the world in ways different from the ways I do. I expected skepticism.

Jung described these experiences as synchronicity—something beyond mere coincidence.

Walter surprised me.

He said God reveals himself and his plan to us each in His own way.

Alec Letter 6

My Loving Son,

Our hearts ache for you.

I hope you know how much we love you. If prayers reach Heaven, surely God will let you hear mine.

We told you every day that we loved you. I hope you heard us in the din of this world. We meant it from the depths of our being.

I believe you are in Heaven in the arms of God, and you are in a place without pain and suffering.

I should rejoice. I was not yet ready to give you up, my son. You were too precious to me.

You were a wonderful son, Alec. A father could not have asked for more. With the exception of the times you hurt yourself through your sports, you were everything I could have hoped for. Those injuries and surgeries! I felt the pain ten times as much as you. So much I loved you and wanted to protect you!

We miss you, Alec.

I miss that gorgeous smile—the one you blessed me with the day you were born.

I miss your strong hugs from that big, beautiful body of yours.

I miss your beautiful fingers, and the delicate hair on your arms.

I miss you waking us up at night when you come in late, and the dog hopping up when he hears your car.

I miss you sprawled on the couch. I miss the smell of your hair, and those beautiful deep eyes.

Your friends have been here to keep us company. They are wonderful kids—you chose well. You chose well on many things.

I was not ready to give you up.

I wanted to watch you grow and use those wonderful talents.

I wanted to see you graduate, marry and have children.

I wanted you to know the joys you brought to me as a father—for you to know the depth of love only a child can teach to a parent.

I wanted to grow old watching you, being proud of you, loving you.

I know Heaven is filled with joy and glory. Does God have equivalents of the good and joyful things we have on earth?

I did not want you to miss these things in life. They are good and wondrous.

You would have been an awesome dad. You would have been a wonderful and loving husband. You would have been a man others would consider themselves lucky to know.

I mostly want to know that you have not missed anything that is good and precious. You deserved to have so much. You loved life and you lived it to the fullest. I wanted you to have as many helpings as you could hold.

I have asked God to assure me of this—that He has time for you. The He will provide you as much as I would as your father. That He will love you, guide you and protect you. That He will look upon you and be as proud of you as I would be. That He will find the time for you that I had planned on spending with you, and savor every moment.

I was not ready to give you up.

I was not yet finished being your father.

Spiritual Journey

Dear Friend,

This is a spiritual journey we are on. We will not be allowed to turn back.

More miracles have come. The contacts, the messages, the phenomena are all beyond the comprehension and dimensions of this physical world we know. But, I know they are real—and others continue to reinforce that.

If they are real, then the spiritual world exists, beyond our senses and understanding. If the spiritual world exists, then your son and mine, both passed, exist within it. And, if they exist there, then we have reason to believe we will be re-united with them again some day. Are we still united? If so, how do we manage to recognize that without the faculties to do so?

Faith is not enough when it comes to your child. I need to hold him. I need to watch him grow. We nurtured and loved him so intently, so intentionally. He was as much a part of my life as any organ in my body, and my body and spirit do not function normally without him.

I remember someone saying how incredible it was to be there for his child's birth because you love your child so instantly—and no one prepared him for this. You don't fall in love with your child like you do with your spouse. You simply and fundamentally love him.

A friend of mine said that she thinks when we die

we will find out that the purpose of life is much simpler than we think it is—that human nature wants to make it more complex than it really needs to be. Emmanuel says it is simply about love.

Alec taught me more about love than I could have ever imagined. I can't imagine he completed that lesson—there was so much more that could have been.

Martin Buber

Dear Alec,

I began to read Buber's *I and Thou*—your philosophy book from school last year. I can see why you enjoyed his writing so much.

"Man's world is manifold, and his attitudes are manifold. What is manifold is often frightening because it is not neat and simple. Men prefer to forget how many possibilities are open to them."

"They like to be told that there are two worlds and two ways. This is comforting because it is so tidy. Wisdom offers simple schemes, but truth is not so simple."[5]

This is our current dilemma, isn't it? We recognize life and death—being and non-being. You seem to be teaching us that there are more options. I remember asking about where I find the truth of God—that truth which is not so simple.

Show me the way, Alec. Show me the way to truth.

Near the Anniversary

Near the anniversary of Alec's death, a friend asked what I had learned in the past year.

Without a moment's thought I answered, "I survived."

It was not a declaration of triumph. It was a statement of fact—imbued with the disbelief, struggle and pain that had been our reality of the year past.

I had survived the thing I thought I could never survive, the thing I would not want to survive. I survived via some unseen force that life seeks and grasps for—some base instinct that overrides consciousness, broken hearts and shattered souls.

From the moment your child is born, you enter a new reality—a new kind of love that cannot be equaled in any other relationship. The future suddenly has more dimensions, more possibility, more reason for hope than it ever had. There is suddenly the awareness of the potential of eternity with this new life—a new generation that has the potential to create and create and create. Each new parent has entered a continuity of life that he/she could not have even imagined without the miracle of this birth.

Life is supposed to work according to the natural rules of succession.

The death of your child is a violation.

I see images of rendering—purification through heat and fire. I have been rendered this year—my soul on fire, the stuff of my innards being separated by the flames of grief. Consciousness is altered. Senses are numbed. Joy is burned from your soul. But you survive.

What now for this purified soul?

Paris

My Dear Alec,

I see you in Paris, my son!

I see you joy-filled walking along the Seine, shouting, "I love Paris! Paris was made just for me!"

It was, my love. It was made *just* for you. It is the dream I created for you before you were even born. It was my gift to you that you should be so completely happy. Paris is yours, my son—and I will join you there again some day.

I love you, Alec. I am only a heartbeat away.

Praise

My Dear Alec,

C.S. Lewis writes that we should praise you.

"Praise is the mode of love which always has some element of joy in it. Praise is in due order; of Him as the giver, of her as the gift. Don't we in praise somehow enjoy what we praise, however far we are from it?"[6]

Of Him as the giver, of you as the gift.

I think of how seldom people speak of you, for fear of hurting us.

We need to speak of you more—to praise you for who you were, for what you did with your life. To praise Him for giving you to us, however short the time.

In Praise — To Know Alec

Alec savored life. He had a zest for it—a sense of exploration, endless fascination, curiosity and love of discovery.

He loved being with other people, dogs and iguanas. He loved the outdoors, changes in the weather and speed. He loved to escape gravity for its sense of freedom—via his snowboard, skateboard, and water skis. He loved playing soccer. And, he loved his red Acura GSR.

Alec was earthly focused, but not earthly bound.

He was quiet with a deep, private spirituality.

He loved Paris—its street life, its night life, history, architecture, atmosphere and essence. I never saw him happier than when he was in Paris.

Alec was a photographer. The camera recorded the unique sights and moments of beauty that he saw, but he valued photography more for what it helped him to see. It was not an aesthetic interest as much as it was an extension of his senses.

Alec took a night shot of the Eiffel Tower one evening when we were in Paris. The Tower was aglow with lights. The time release and just a bit of movement made the picture a tower of stars. He submitted this photo into a competition and received recognition for its merit. He treasured this photo. It was one of a very few he left on my computer just before he died.

Alec felt a special closeness to his extended family, and cherished our times together. He loved Christmas and all of its traditions. When he was very little, he asked us to buy a crèche with the Christ Child separate from the manager, so he "could hold Baby Jesus." Each year it was his job to decorate the mantle with the nutcracker collection. And, he loved mice. No telling why, but he loved them. A stuffed toy of Jerry, from Tom and Jerry, was with him always until he went to school.

He was very proud of his Celtic heritage. It provided roots for him—a sense of connectedness to his past, and perhaps future. He understood the struggles of his forebears, and did not take his history or his present for granted. His favorite movie was *Braveheart*—he felt a kinship with the injustices, the struggles and victories documented in that movie.

When he turned 18, Alec had a Celtic cross tattooed on his back. His college application essay was beautifully written on the meaning of his tattoo—representing his faith, his heritage and his commitments.

He later had a Celtic Trinity knot tattooed on his arm. The knot was in memory of two friends who were killed in an auto accident in the spring of 2002. The third point was in memory of the victims of the September 11, 2001 attacks. He was very disturbed by both events. When visiting New York in December 2001, he was profoundly moved by the views of the site of the former World Trade Center.

Alec was sensitive to the tragedy in life. He felt a connectedness to human kind.

Alec was a collector—no, more of a "treasurer" of things. He was more appreciative than materialistic. He had a sense of wonderment about things. They were touchstones of his experiences and his relationships—reflections of love. He had drawers full of notes from friends, trinkets from trips, gifts from his grandmother—each bit treasured as much as another.

In many ways, Alec was just a normal kid, but he had an extraordinary nature. People were drawn to him. People liked being with him. He had an amazingly kind heart.

Alec had a smile which would light up a room. From the day he was born, he smiled at us and at the world. It was instinctive for him to smile.

If there is any one thing he should be remembered by, it is his smile.

Personal Statement

Alec Lloyd Robinson
College Application Essay

Zzzzzzzz. The noise of the tattoo needle was only drowned out by the blaring rock music being blasted from the tiny gray radio on the shelf. I was in a small white room, much like a doctor's office, but hung with sketches and photos of art rather than diagrams of ligaments and bone structures. I sat as still as I possibly could as a guy I had just met went diligently to work adorning the flesh on my back with his black ink. "Wow," I thought, "I'm really here, getting a tattoo." It was my eighteenth birthday.

As I sat in that chair, in a fairly uncomfortable position, I pondered how my parents and friends would react to the Celtic cross that was being permanently emblazoned on my shoulder blade. These thoughts were not new to me. I had thought a great deal about it ever since I had proclaimed to my parents, at the age of fifteen, that I was going to get a tattoo of a cross when I was old enough. "Why would you want to deface your perfect body with a tattoo?" they would ask. "You're going to regret it when you're older." Obviously I did not heed their warnings. Sure, I might have regretted getting certain things tattooed on my body, useless, unimportant things that would have no meaning to me when my youth has turned into a more mature and conservative adulthood. But the tattoo I got is not like that; it is a self-designed cross, which represents three things to me—ideals that I hold dear and will never be ashamed to bear the mark of. The first is my heritage. I am very proud of my Scottish roots; my cross is a reminder of those roots and of the sacrifices made by all of my ancestors, all the way up to my parents, so that I may live the life I live today. Second is my attitude towards life. I try to live every day to the fullest. Getting a tattoo just augmented my attitude of "Carpe Diem." Third and most importantly, my cross represents my faith. As a Christian, the cross is a constant reminder to me that my life was bought at a price, that it is not mine but the Lord's to do with as He will. It is also a daily and permanent proclamation of my faith, and helps remind me of how I should live.

Fifty years from now people may look at the wrinkly knot-work and fading image of my cross and think it looks like a tacky thing I did when I was young and stupid. But I will look at it and be happy, because it will remind me of my youth, of those who sacrificed so much for me, and of a faith that is so important to me.

Tears

I have cried every day for a year for this son.
365 days of tears.
Tears for the void of Alec in our lives.
Tears for the horror we've endured.
Tears for the pain in his mother's eyes.
Tears for the tenderness and compassion of his friends.
Tears for the unanswered questions to God and man.
Tears for the moments we will never have.
In truth, we recall our lives in moments—broken leg,
   first kiss, marriage vows, birth of child, death of
   loved one.
There will be so many moments we will never have.
Never again four of us in a family photo.
Never again a Christmas without a shadow.
Never again those anticipatory smiles.
Never the joy of his wedding day.
Never his pride in handing us his first child.
Never the opportunity to confide in his brother secrets
   which only brothers share.
Never the chance to be his brother's best man.
Never the exhilaration of snow boarding down the
   Rockies.
I see these moments every day in my life and the life
   of others, and I think, "we'll never have that with
   Alec"—no matter how insignificant it may seem.
So many "never moments" worthy of tears.

His Room

People offered to clean out his room that first week. Oh, to have him ripped from our lives twice so quickly!

There is essence of him there: scents of him, how he organized his life, the things he treasured.

There are those who could use his clothes. Yes. But, so can we.

Are we holding on? Yes, oh yes!

But I keep my grandfather's watch, and my father's graduation pin, and my teddy bear and the tie from my wedding. Essences. It is human to hold on.

We had him for nearly 20 years. There is no reason to rush now.

I will give money to the poor, blood to the sick, time to the needy. These are resources which are renewable.

His essence is now finite.

Christmas Ornaments

How many things we take for granted and silently assume in our lives.

As I decorate the Christmas tree I look at these ornaments passed down from my grandfather that I assumed would become his.

It was part of his history, his future, his gift to his children.

We never spoke of these.

A parent carries many silent gifts in his heart.

Jacob

I have come to Japan in the tradition of Jacob.

I have come to wrestle with God.

In this realm of Kami and Buddha, might I find some advantage?

In the Sumo ring, purified with salt, I will confront Him, I will defy Him with the full weight of my sorrow.

"Why?" I will demand.

"Because."

"Why him, this most precious one?!"

"Because I know best.

"Why me? Why us?"

"Because it is not yet time for you to understand."

I remember resenting my earthly father for his smugness and his intransigence—until one day I heard his words come from my own mouth.

How old will I need to be before I understand this time?

I have already aged so.

If I prevail, will God bless me?

If so, what will that blessing be?

Two Mice

My Dear Son,

Two mice peeked out of a shop window at me today.

You would have loved them—made by hand from an antique silk kimono.

I bought them as a reminder of you—of your joy.

Even with a tear in my eye, I can take one step in the dance of your life.

Breakfast Today

My Dear Alec,

I have heard others criticized for not moving on after the death of their child—of always clinging to what will never be.

Grief is complex—it hides in secret corners and under rocks within the soul—emerging when least expected, wearing the masks of other emotions.

I have found some peace here in Japan, some newer degree of acceptance.

But, there were two handsome young couples seated next to me at breakfast this morning with their guidebooks to Kyoto, excited and anticipatory. How jealous I was that that will never be you—here again to explore and savor.

We move on, we who have lost a child. We just do it with a sense of incompletion amidst the abundance of life.

And we never stop loving.

Ray

Ray is our minister.

I love Ray.

He is a compassionate, kind, learned and wise man. I joined his congregation because he has shepherded an incredible group of individuals into an extraordinary flock of caring and giving people.

After JoRoyce called me to tell me Alec had died, I could only think of one person I wanted to be at our house. If I could not be there, it was Ray. Ray would provide comfort. Ray would know what to do. Directory Assistance could not find his number. I desperately called a friend whom I knew could reach him. I did not get to speak to him that night. But he went to the house, and in that I found some peace.

Ray is a big man. He was a football star in college. When he is in our house the ceilings seem to descend a few inches. At 5 ft. 5 in., I see his hands better than I see his face. He has big hands, strong hands, hands which have worked and hands which can be ever so gentle. He uses those hands to greet people and welcome friends— to bless the heads of children at church—to securely hold those he baptizes.

The last words Ray said at the funeral were, "Alec Lloyd Robinson, rest in the arms of God," and he commended him to God. I could see Ray ever so gently passing my son to a loving and waiting God with those big, strong, gentle football hands. And, I was so grateful.

Pieta.

Not long after the funeral we went to see Ray for guidance. We met him in his office, filled with books, ancient and new, which discussed and analyzed God, life, and religion. Certainly there would be answers here—this big man of God who stood closer to Heaven than we, and these many, many sources.

We asked the reverberating question of every parent, "Why?" Ray told he had no answers in situations like this. After so many years in the ministry, God had never answered his questions about why children die. We asked about the experiences we had had. Ray could only answer, "Listen to your life."

As we left that day, Ray seemed smaller, wearier—more like the rest of us, wandering through rocky grasslands, bleating into the void of the universe.

Part II

Miracles

When I Said Goodbye

When I said goodbye to my son for the last time, I asked for a gift—a sign from him that he was with God and safe. The only way I knew I could live with his death was to know he was safe.

It is not without some significant irony that I, who have ranted and railed against death and God over the past two years, now write the words to follow here—that I become a messenger about experiences I cannot explain, nor fully understand, yet find profoundly meaningful and significant.

How does one write about the inexplicable and the incomprehensible? I have decided to do it simply and directly.

I know confidently that have I received my gift from Alec, many times over. Since he died, we have experienced so many "events," to an extent that should be described as extraordinary. We have shared these with family, close friends and others who have endured painful loss of loved ones, only to find that others have had similar experiences.

It is difficult to write about these. First, they are intimate and extremely personal. Second, to discuss them beyond close family and friends makes one vulnerable to the reaction, assumptions and ignorance of others. We have found that very few people are willing to discuss such phenomena openly, for fear of appearing crazy or desperately needy. We live in a culture of reason, demanding scientific proof. We struggle when we try to explain things we do not understand fully.

Individually, the events we describe in the following pages could be explained away as weird coincidences. Collectively, they create a body of experience which is impossible to ignore.

Are these miracles? They feel miraculous. But, that word has many connotations which might unfairly complicate this dialogue. I cannot explain how they happen, only that they are real.

The most often recurring events involve coins. Coins have appeared consistently in the most unexpected and inexplicable places, particularly when we have traveled or there has been a family experience where Alec's presence was greatly missed, or some assurance of a remaining connection is welcome. A few of these experiences are recounted here, but there are far too many to try to include them all. There is no routine or pattern, but within our family and close friends, there have been more than 200 incidences of coins appearing where they should not, or where they are clearly intended to catch one's attention. These include pennies, dimes, nickels and quarters. There is no predicting the appearance of the coins and you cannot "will" them to appear. It does no good to ask for one, and if you look for one, you can almost guarantee there will not be one.

There have also been events related to electronic devices—primarily related to computers and music. Dreams have long been thought to be ways spirits communicate with us. I recount three dreams here, from three different people—all of which had special meaning, unusual character and memorable quality to their "dreamers."

I have been particularly blessed with these contacts, as has my mother, who was very close to Alec. But, I include the experiences of many others who have been generous enough to share their stories. We have discussed with close friends the source of these contacts—are they from Alec, angels, or God himself? It has been almost amusing that we have found strong opinion about this—as though any of us could know. In the end, it does not matter, for ultimately they reflect miraculous intervention and intentional acts to contact and comfort.

We are ordinary people living ordinary lives. Had you asked me two years ago if I believed such experiences were possible, I would have responded as a skeptic. I have tried many times to explain them away, only to have them reoccur and reinforce their continued presence in our lives. I have tried to make "sense" out of what seems incredible. I have come to a point where I know I do not understand how this world works, and that there are dimensions we neither see nor comprehend.

I have come to accept them with awe, wonderment, mystery and thanksgiving, even though those emotions are always accompanied by recurrent pain in the loss they also represent. One of my greatest challenges since Alec's death has been to find a way to integrate these experiences into our lives—to find acceptance of both death and miracles into my reality, neither of which had I been prepared to embrace.

I asked a theologian friend how he would characterize these experiences. His response was that he considers it a "sin to underestimate the power of God."

I have felt compelled to document our experiences—to compile them and share them in hopes they will provide a context for others. About the time I made a commitment to find a way to undertake this task, a friend submitted my name as a candidate for a new grant program. As a 2005 recipient, I was blessed with the opportunity to take a short sabbatical from my regular career to focus on this writing. The day before Alec's 22nd birthday, as I sat thinking about how I could honor him—what I could still give to my son—I received a call, that very moment, telling me I had been selected to receive the grant.

This is my gift.

I spent a month in Kyoto, Japan, using the gardens there for reflection and inspiration. Immersed in a culture which values meditation and introspection, in the serenity of the green hills of the city, with memories of a past visit there with Alec when he was just nine years old, surrounded by the courtesy and grace of the Japanese people, I contemplated and wrote.

These are some of our most distinct and memorable events—indeed, not all of them. They are shared to give voice to this human experience which, as yet, remains mostly mute. And, while the intent of this writing is not to establish any religious doctrine, it is ultimately a statement of hope and faith.

Ray advised us, "Listen to your life." We share our experiences in reverence of the unseen—told in love and gratitude. These are a part of Alec's legacy, and a continuation of his love and impact on our lives.

Baum

"Never question the truth of what you fail to understand, for the world is filled with wonders."[7]

L. Frank Baum

The Miracles

It wasn't long before JoRoyce, Ian and I were aware that strange things were happening to us. We knew we were under tremendous duress, and the logical thing was to question everything. We were coping to get from minute to minute.

But, as we look back, the miracles began almost immediately.

As soon as the police officers left our house that Tuesday night, Ian went to his room, stunned to have heard his brother had died. The only thing he could think of was to call some of his close friends—he knew he needed their presence and support. As he re-entered his room his CD player was playing. He had not had it on for two days, but now it was playing music—the second track of a CD by Mercy Me, the song "I Can Only Imagine." It was a song about the experience of seeing God's face for the first time. He had no idea of how it had come on.

I was on a business trip. When my cell phone rang in my motel room—in the dresser drawer—it surprised me. It was after midnight. I always turn my cell phone off at night to save the battery. I had already checked in at home. All was well. I had rushed up to New York late that afternoon to join a tour program, and had just managed to join the group for dinner at 8:00. Someone asked about my family, and I remember describing Alec at college as a "bon vivant," and then thinking it was an odd choice of words, not sure of where that came from. It was probably about 8:20—the time of his accident.

The next morning, amidst the chaos, JoRoyce found three quarters on the carpet of the family room, just sitting out in the open. She assumed they fell out of one of the kids' pockets. No big deal, but she did remember it as odd.

My parents came to Richmond immediately. They stayed with our good friends and neighbors. The first morning there, Mom found a dime in the middle of the bathroom floor. That same evening, Dad found a dime in the street, shining in the evening light.

Alec's personal possessions were returned to us sometime in the first few days. There wasn't much other than his wallet, his watch, a cross he always wore, and a bunch of quarters. He had no bills in his wallet, and 12 quarters in his pocket. I remember thinking how strange—quarters had become a joke between Alec and me. He never did his laundry at college, and routinely dragged home bags of it when he came home on weekends. I remember asking him why he never did laundry at school. He told me it was because he never had quarters—an apparently insurmountable problem for my college freshman. I began to save quarters for him.

The day we buried Alec, as I kissed him goodbye I could hardly leave him. I made a mental note to myself about the way he smelled. He smelled so good to me—a sweet, spicy, waxy fragrance that I knew I would never forget. JoRoyce thought my behavior was very odd. I silently told him that I needed a sign from him to know that he was all right—that I could not live with his loss without some reassurance that he was with God. I began to place a photo in his coffin which he had taken on our family vacation in Paris—a night shot of the Eiffel Tower which had special meaning for him. At the last moment, I put it back into my pocket. It was too precious a memory to bury with him. I told him I would picture him in Paris. If there was a Heaven, Paris would be as close as I could imagine. I had never seen him happier and more excited about life. Paris could be Heaven for Alec.

By Sunday afternoon people were taking their leave. As we chatted and reminisced in the living room, I was aware that I was surrounded by the fragrance of Alec in those last few minutes with him on Friday. I felt like I was hallucinating. I was disoriented and frightened—and excused myself to go upstairs for a few minutes. After trying to pull myself together and washing my face with cold water, I looked in the mirror and had this sudden revelation—the fragrance was that of lilies. Alec had smelled like lilies.

The living room was filled with lilies in arrangements which had been sent in remembrance and comfort. But most importantly, the very first flower to arrive was a lily, and it was from our friend named Hope.

Had my son found a way to reassure his father, the horticulturist, that he was OK through the fragrance of lilies?

I was either losing my mind or something very real and very powerful was happening.

I could not help but call Hope and tell her my experience. I was overwhelmed, and doubting my sanity, but I wanted her to hear this story.

She told me she was amazed that I was calling because buying the lilies had become a "big deal" for her.

Hope heard the news about Alec early on Wednesday, and she said she felt an immediate need to express her support, and wanted to send flowers to us.

She went to the florist personally to choose something, and the only thing she saw that attracted her eye were some pink lilies. She selected the stems and went to pay for them, but the register was staffed by two young girls who were in the midst of gossiping, oblivious to her standing there wanting to pay. Hope said she felt such an urgency to get the flowers to us that she became incensed. Finally, the transaction was complete, and a bit unnerved, she was on her way to bring the flowers to the house.

That evening, she couldn't get out of her mind the strength of her emotion early in the day—and she had been trying to analyze her reaction. She knew it had been out of character, even given the circumstances, but, she knew she had felt so strongly that she had to get the lilies to us.

She said none of it had made sense, until I told her about the fragrance of the lilies and my linking it to Alec and some sense of reassurance that he was OK. I have since called these the lilies from Hope.

"Listen to your life," said Ray. "Listen to your life."

Coins

There is no explaining the coins. They just show up, and they show up directly in your path or field of vision where you cannot miss them.

They appear on the road when we walk, they appear in the car at auspicious times (our car and others'). They appear in luggage when we travel. One (an American penny) even showed up in the Frankfurt Germany airport when JoRoyce went into the ladies' room. When coming home from a trip to New York City, several appeared on the street behind our car between loads of luggage. They appear in parking lots, almost always on the ground right at the driver's door.

They have appeared in a showroom at the wholesale gift mart in Atlanta after sharing a story about them, and on the carpet of a friend when she arrived home after remembering Alec on a trip.

They appear on the aisles of airplanes, and in hotel rooms. They appear in my pockets. After my mother asked me to place a bright Haitian lizard on Alec's grave, because she could not find an iguana, she discovered pennies under her old-fashioned footed bathtub—one Alec loved and thought was so "cool." They have appeared time after time on my mother's washing machine, and they have appeared overnight on the stairs of her house. As an alternative, occasionally paperclips appear as well. I cannot explain why, other than I have loved paperclips since I was a child, and like duct tape, I can make or fix almost anything with a paperclip. These appear where you would not expect to find paperclips, and like the coins, they seem strategically placed.

We traveled to Italy for two weeks the summer of 2005, and the entire time there was no sense of connection. Then one day in Capri, as we visited an old estate, we found "Carpe Diem" (Alec's motto) inscribed in the floor of the dining room, (the first time it was referenced during our time in Italy), and as we left, there was a paperclip right in the middle of the walkway as we exited. The estate was named San Michele—the same as the district of Paris that Alec loved so much!

Coins have shown up in Alec's sneakers, two years after he died. And, in a file folder of maps, which had not been opened for years, when I went to retrieve maps to take to Japan, there sat a shiny, singular dime.

They are intentional. At times, they seem interactive. They certainly seem intended to be comforting and connecting—little hellos, and reminders that he is not far away. As a friend of mine said—they get your attention.

"Listen to your life," said Ray.

The First Week of Coincidences

The day after the accident, Alec's friends created a memorial at the crash site. They posted pictures, cards, and mementoes of their times together. People brought flowers, and neighbors in the area left messages of condolences and encouragement. There was almost a constant vigil there for days.

Chris was one of Alec's best friends. He is funny and sometimes crazy, and has a heart of gold. Alec loved Chris for Chris always made him laugh. Chris is a very big young man, strong and athletic. But, he is not always as cautious as he should be. He had a bad habit of steering his car with his knees, so that he could have his hands free to talk on his cell phone, reach for the CD player, eat, etc. He always had his steering wheel set very low, so his knees could be in contact with it. One afternoon, when he went to the crash site, he left his car parked along the road. After spending a few minutes with the other kids he returned to his car. No-one else had been in his car, but when he got in, his steering wheel was raised in a normal driving position. His knees could not touch the wheel, as they always did. He told us he had this strange sense that Alec was telling him to drive more safely—which he immediately began to do.

Whitney was Alec's girlfriend. He loved spending time at Whit's house with her parents, Bev and Ted. Alec adored them all. The week after the funeral, Ted spent much of one day cleaning Whitney's car. It was a way to keep busy. He thoroughly cleaned both the outside and inside, including vacuuming and treating all the seats with conditioner. Just a few minutes after completing the job, Ted decided to move the car from the driveway. When he climbed into the driver's seat, there was a bright penny in the passenger seat—one he was sure had not been there when he had finished the cleaning job.

Alec had played soccer for 11 years, and for the majority of those had the same coaches who co-led the team, Neil and Steve. He was close to both of them, and they were each fathers of two of his school friends.

One of those coaches, Neil, is a practicing psychiatrist. He very kindly came several times to sit with us and to spend time visiting. One evening, he was discussing some of his cases, and mentioned something about delusional thinking. I asked if we could talk about "delusions," and shared with him some of the strange events that seemed to be taking place. I asked Neil if he thought I were delusional. He quickly said, "No." When I asked him what he thought was going on, he told me that he believed in the possibility of some connection from the world of the dead, or direct communication from God. He noted that there is incident after incident in the Old Testament where God communicates directly with man. Only in our more scientific era over the past century or so have we decided that this is not possible, nor plausible.

After citing a few of the experiences we had had in the past few days, Neil exclaimed, "My Gosh! Now maybe I have an answer as to what happened to my car last week!" The prior weekend, Neil was scheduled to play a tournament game with his adult soccer team. He did not feel well, and he was not motivated to play, but he did not want to let his team down. He drove to the field, parked and locked his car along the street, and went on to play the game. Neil's team, against all expectation, won the game. Neil said he had thought about Alec all through the game—of his competitive spirit and his love of winning. At the end of the game, he lifted the trophy and silently said, "This is for you, Alec."

When he got back to his car, and climbed in, his steering wheel was in a different position, the seat had been moved back, and the back of the seat was significantly reclined. Neil was sure the car was locked, but asked a couple of friends around if they had been in his car for some reason. They all assured him they had not been, and had not seen anyone in it. Neil said when he sat in the seat, he was halfway lying down, and had to extend his arms to reach the wheel.

We were stunned. That is exactly the position in which Alec always drove. We used to tease him that he looked like a pimp driving around semi-reclined like that.

And then, we learned that Neil's car was exactly the same model, color and year of my car—the car Alec was driving when he died.

Steve was another special friend to Alec and to our family. He was obviously very distressed about Alec's death. We told Steve about some of the unusual things that had happened to us, particularly the appearance of the pennies. Steve is a very devout man. I am not sure what he thought at first. In a couple of weeks he came back to see us with a story of his own.

One evening while his wife was away, Steve decided to do some chores around the house. His wife had given him a new tool box as a Christmas gift, which he had used many times since he had received it. He got it out to prepare for his work. When he opened it, he was stunned to find in the center of the top divided tray, a single shiny penny staring at him. He said he knew each and every tool in that toolbox, and there was no explaining why a penny was suddenly there. He and his wife had never put one there. He was sure it came as a small "hello" from Alec.

Replacing the Car

Alec was in my car when he had the accident. It is an irony, for I bought it because it was big, heavy, well built and had all the latest safety features. I bought it because it was safe. In his case none of that mattered.

After the accident, everything about cars was repulsive. We heard too many stories about kids who died in wrecks. We never thought we would be facing this—we had been so safety conscious about vehicles to protect ourselves and the kids. We thought we had minimized our risks.

About a month after the accident, we planned to join JoRoyce's family at the beach. I felt compelled to get the business of replacing the car complete before we left town. We did not need it for transport at that point. I just wanted to get it behind us. The reality of a new car was part of the reality that Alec wasn't coming home. I hated it, but I did not want to prolong it either.

I knew the people at the dealership and trusted them. They knew about the accident and had been very sympathetic. I explained that we needed to make this as simple and painless as possible. I would choose the model and color; they would work out the paperwork to complete the deal. Two steps—done.

I asked for a white vehicle. Unfortunately, they did not have one in stock. The salesman called to ask if I would come to the lot and make a choice from what was available. Car shopping, even if for only choosing a color, was the last thing I wanted to do. I asked them to select another color, prep it for me to test drive and have the paperwork ready to sign. They called when the car was ready.

When I arrived at the dealership, Sean, the salesman, said that they had my car for me, and proudly pulled a white vehicle around the corner of the showroom. I asked where it had come from, and he said it had just come in. I did the requisite test drive. As we left the lot, I noticed the car had exactly 9 miles on the odometer. Sean noted that this was very unusual—most cars had more miles than that just from test drives and transport. This one was truly brand new.

I asked that we expedite the paperwork. As it was being processed, Sean told me that they were going to deliver the car to the house that evening. I said it would be fine to leave it on the lot until we returned in a week. Sean apologetically explained that for insurance reasons once the car was sold, they preferred to get it off their lot. He assured me that it would be totally unobtrusive.

Just as we completed the deal, several new customers arrived in the showroom. Soon Sean was in front of me explaining there was no-one to follow him and pick him up when he delivered the car to our house. "Would I mind quickly driving him back." Yes, I minded. I was exhausted by now, both physically and emotionally. The last thing I wanted to do was spend more time getting the car home, and making a round trip to deliver the salesman back to the dealership. But, I was too tired to argue, and conceded to give him a ride

When we got to the house, I quickly parked and went

to join Sean in the new car. I hoped we would ride in silence. But, he quickly began to talk, asking if he could share something with me. "Mr. Robinson, I have been selling cars for a long time, and I have to tell you this sale is the most unusual of my career. It is like this car was meant to be yours. None of the salesmen knew it was on the lot—our manager had traded it for a red one someone wanted, and it just appeared. None of us knew it was there. It was exactly what you requested, and it was just sitting there when I went to double check our stock. I have just had this strange feeling about it, and I had to tell you."

I thought how odd. He had never mentioned anything before this opportunity when we were alone. Had he not insisted on delivering the car, had the flurry of customers not come in at the end of the day, none of this last conversation would have taken place. I never would have known about these unusual circumstances.

About a month later, I returned to the dealership to pick up the license plates. Sean was there, and said he hoped we liked the vehicle. He had continued to think about the odd circumstances of it, and he said he felt like it was just the right car for us—"angelic white."

I noticed a sign on the wall, which announced Sean had been salesman of the month for July. I congratulated him, asking how many vehicles he had sold. It was substantial, so I asked what number in the sequence had our vehicle been. He said it was the ninth vehicle he sold in July.

Alec's lucky number was 9.

Frank's Dream

A few weeks after Alec died, I had a very vivid dream one night—one with a quality that is unlike any other dream I have ever had in my life. The details are so distinct, the experience so real, and the memory of it provides a sense of peace and comfort.

I was working in my garden—in the east side of our back yard, near the white Lilac 'Pride of Rochester.' (Alec was born in Rochester, NY.) I looked up and Alec was walking toward me from around the corner of the house. He looked young, healthy, calm, and was smiling that incredible smile of his. I was so happy to see him. Without getting up from my knees, I looked up at him and asked very carefully and calmly, "Are you OK?"

"Yes, Dad."

And then, "Is all well?"

"Yes, Dad."

And a third time, "Are you content?"

"Yes, Dad."

After this brief sequence, I stood up and picked up some litter from the garden in my left hand, and, a pair of Alec's work boots, (which appeared from nowhere), in my right hand. I then walked to the south edge of the garden, while Alec stood in the same place behind me.

As I reached the edge of the garden, I walked into

magnificent, bright light, and I placed Alec's boots and the garden debris into the light.

There, the dream ended, but I had this calm sense that Alec *is* OK, and that his "work" on earth is completed.

The Beach

JoRoyce's family had a tradition of gathering at the beach each summer. For years her parents generously rented a cottage right on the water, where we all spent a week together. The kids could bring friends. There are many memorable moments from those weeks.

In 2003 the trip was scheduled for just three weeks after Alec died. Despite our devastation, we all decided to continue with the reunion. It would not be the same, but it might be good to put ourselves into a new environment for a few days.

We arrived late on check-in day—after 8:00 P.M. It was June 21, the summer solstice. We went through the traditional choosing of rooms, moving in luggage, and running to the grocery store for staples for that night and the next morning. It was nearly 1:00 A.M. before we were all settled, and we were desperate to go to bed. Suddenly, Karen suggested that we three have a cup of herbal tea on the deck overlooking the ocean before we call it a night. We protested, but Karen insisted, putting water on to boil. It was easier to give in.

We went out to sit in the black night, the ocean's roar and the smell of the surf engulfing us. Suddenly there appeared on the horizon the oddest round red glow. We thought at first it might be a satellite, but its orbit was moving straight up from the sea. It was a red star, and our best guess was that it was Mars.

Without time to process a thought, I heard myself saying, "I knew we would have a sign from Alec!" JoRoyce looked at me and asked what I was talking about. I replied, "The Eiffel Tower sits on the Champs de Mars in Paris!" Somewhere in the back of my brain, I knew this, but I had not had a conscious thought about the Champs de Mars in years. There was this "instant knowing," and I had no doubt the link to the Eiffel Tower photo and Paris was intentional. It turned out that Mars rose that night on the east coast about 1:11 A.M. It was closer to the earth in 2003 than it had been in 70,000 years. We just happened to be sitting on the front deck of the beach house looking east into the night when it appeared, because Karen wanted to have a cup of tea. Otherwise, we would been asleep, oblivious to its presence.

Alec loved the Eiffel Tower. It had become symbolic of his joy and passion for life. His photographs captured its light—and the thrill he had the first night he saw it in Paris. Paris is where I promised to picture him in my mind. If I could not have him with me, I would have him in Paris. The Champs de Mars was as irrelevant as anything could be in our lives that night on the beach. But, suddenly the faint red glow of Mars reflected so much in our lives.

The house we stayed in that week was a bit funky—older, darker, more worn than houses we had been in previous years. In the dining area there was a large Audubon print of a blue heron. It seemed to be in my direct sight-line whenever I sat at the dinner table. I remember thinking it was an oddly sophisticated element in what was otherwise a pretty ordinary rented vacation house. But, there it was.

When we returned from the beach we found an e-mail from Ann, one of our longest and dearest friends. In her message she told us of how she had thought of us over the past weeks. She was unable to come to the funeral, but hoped we knew she was with us in spirit. On the day of Alec's funeral, it was pouring rain in Connecticut where she lived. She said she could not sit still, emotions spilling over. She felt too confined in the house with her thoughts, so she decided to take a drive, in spite of the weather. Through tears and the downpour of rain she found herself on a road she did not know—one that ended at a small pond. There she sat, crying for us, crying for Alec—watching a beautiful blue heron feeding along the water's edge. And somehow, the heron brought her peace.

It turned out that we stayed at the Platt cottage that summer. Our friend who brought the first lilies to us after learning of Alec's death is also named Platt.

The experience of Mars, and the Champs de Mars, led me to research on the internet. Mars was the god of war in Roman mythology—thus the Champs de Mars next to the war college in Paris, on which the Eiffel Tower was built. In addition, the planet Mars has a bright, vast area on its northern hemisphere known as "The Elysian Fields." As one thing leads to another, after reading about the Champs de Mars, I explored the significance of the Elysian Fields, and the Champs de Lyscee, that spectacularly famous avenue in Paris. Champs means "field." Lyscee means Elysian.

The Elysian Fields were the Greek "Islands of the Dead"—the place where humans, chosen by the gods, would live in eternity. According to Webster, "a place or condition of ideal happiness," "dwelling place assigned to happy souls after death; Paradise." One reference cited "Isles of the Blest" as a synonym. The "Isles of the Blest" have persisted in Celtic legend as the place where favored souls were received by the gods to live happily in Paradise.

Every path I followed took me back to Alec—his love of Paris, his photo of the Eiffel Tower, his passion for his Celtic heritage, reference to eternity and Paradise—and ideal happiness. The links to our friend Ann and Hope were inexplicable, but so unmistakable.

How many coincidences and links could there be in just a few days time?

Computer Files

We had two computers in our house—the family computer that was to be used by all, and one for a small internet business, which housed our website and received orders. The boys knew they were never to use that computer other than perhaps to do some word processing or quickly check e-mails. Photo files and downloaded songs were forbidden due to my concerns about viruses and insufficient memory available for the website operation.

Alec had created a file on that computer for work he saved for the short term. I paid little attention to it, but after his death, I naturally wanted to see what was there. I was surprised to find photographs and some downloaded music lyrics.

As I explored the files I was struck by two things— 1. They were an odd assortment, and 2. Those that I recognized as his most favorite photographs had all been saved to my computer one evening—April 18 at 8:20 P.M.—the same time as his accident, and the date of his birth.

The photos were all of things with special meaning to Alec, or things that needed taking care of in his absence. These included two items he had sold on eBay, but had not yet shipped to his customers—almost as a reminder to me to follow up for him.

In addition, there were photographs of his brother, whom Alec admired tremendously, his girlfriend, our family Christmas tree, the eternal flame in the Holocaust

Memorial in Paris, and one of the Eiffel Tower—the latter almost identical to a picture I had wanted to put in his coffin (but decided to keep at the last moment).

Perhaps most striking were the lyrics to a song entitled "When You Come Back Down," performed by the group Nickel Creek, a country/bluegrass band. Alec had a wide interest in music, but it was decisively in the vein of Rap and Hard Rock. This song did not fit with anything we knew he listened to. He did at times download lyrics for Whitney, but this song was all about someone who had died and was off to pursue bigger dreams—not the love songs he would send to Whit.

In early July, one of Alec's very good friends, Lauren, came to visit. She told us about taking Whitney to a concert on July 1, to hear Nickel Creek! I asked if Lauren knew the song, "When You Come Back Down," and she said it was one of her favorites. I asked if Whit had been a fan of Nickel Creek. Lauren said Whit had never heard the group until the concert they attended on July 1st.

You cannot read these lyrics without wondering about the intent. Of all the things he could have left on that computer, these words are both haunting, and beautiful—about the need to move on "to chase a dream before it slips away."

Nickel Creek   *(Composed by Danny O'Keefe and Tim O'Brien)*
"When You Come Back Down"

You got to leave me now, you got to go alone
You got to chase a dream, one that's all your own

Before it slips away
When you're flyin' high, take my heart along
I'll be the harmony to every lonely song
That you learn to play

When you're soarin' through the air
I'll be your solid ground
Take every chance you dare
I'll still be there
When you come back down
When you come back down

I'll keep lookin' up, awaitin' your return
My greatest fear will be that you will crash and burn
And I won't feel your fire
I'll be the other hand that always holds the line
Connectin' in between your sweet heart and mine
I'm strung out on that wire
And I'll be on the other end, To hear you when you call
Angel, you were born to fly, If you get too high
I'll catch you when you fall
I'll catch you when you fall

[Bridge:]
Your memory's the sunshine every new day brings
I know the sky is calling
Angel, let me help you with your wings
When you're soarin' through the air
I'll be your solid ground
Take every chance you dare

I'll still be there
When you come back down
Take every chance you dare,
I'll still be there
When you come back down
When you come back down[8]

Computer Links

On July 4th we were invited to join some friends for dinner. The gathering included parents and buddies of Alec. Alec had loved going to their house—this was the hangout where the boys played poker—it was always a fun night out for him.

We got home about 11:00 P.M. I opened my computer to check e-mail. In the lower corner there was an unusual message I had never seen before that said "Check Messages." I clicked the box and a blank screen appeared. There were no messages, so I shut the computer down for the night.

I turned on the family computer to check e-mail on that machine. The Instant Messenger box came up with Alec's ID on it—something that I had not seen since before he had died and he used it routinely. Then, another small box appeared that said "Important New Messages"—again, a box I'd never seen before. I clicked on the box—gray with rounded corners. The enlarged box said, "Bringing you important new messages," with five options on the right side. The bottom box was titled *Pearl Jam*—Alec's favorite band.

I clicked the *Pearl Jam* box and immediately a streaming video began playing "Pearl Jam at the House of Blues, April 18, 2003." (This was the same night that Alec had copied lyrics of "When You Come Back Down" and photo files to my computer.) The song being performed was "Can't Keep."

Pearl Jam *(Composed by Eddie Vedder)*

"Can't Keep"

I wanna shake
I wanna wind out
I wanna leave
This mind and shout

I've lived
All this life
Like an ocean
In disguise
I don't live for
Ever
You can't keep
Me here

I wanna race
With the sundown
I want a last breath
I don't let out.

Forgive
Every being
The bad feelings
It's just me
I won't wait
For answers
You can't keep
Me here

I wanna rise
And say goodnight
Wanna take
A look on the other side

I've lived
All those lives
It's been wonder
Full at night
I will live for
Ever
You can't keep
Me here[9]

A month later, on August 3, 2003, I opened the family computer, and again, the gray "New Message" box appeared. Again, there were five boxes to choose from, but nothing seemed related to Alec in any way. I clicked on one of the boxes and a message said, "Your message will appear after this brief advertisement." A video began of a boy skateboarding, with an ad for video cameras and software to produce action videos. Alec loved making videos of himself and friends skateboarding—we have hours of tape he made.

For me there is no subtlety here. Both events were totally spontaneous, and both totally related to our son, his interests and his passing. Messages from beyond. "I will live forever, you can't keep me here."

Dorothy's Story

Dorothy has been a volunteer at the botanical garden where I've worked for years. We have known each other, but not well. At a volunteer luncheon event, Dorothy expressed her condolences and shared with me that she had lost her son as well, in his thirties, just a couple of years before Alec died—also a totally unexpected death.

Dorothy had heard from another of our volunteers, in whom I had confided a few of my stories, about the pennies appearing. She and asked if I would share some of my experiences with her. In a few minutes she told me that she had been finding pennies in her house ever since her son had died, but had never heard the "Pennies from Heaven" story. She said that she lived totally alone, so to find pennies in odd places had confounded her, until I shared my penny stories with her. She said she thought she had been losing her mind when she found pennies in places where she knew she had not dropped or placed them.

A couple of weeks later, Dorothy made a point to see me and said she had a story I needed to hear. After our prior discussion, she decided she would share her and my experiences with her daughter who lived out west. She said her daughter was a "woman of science," and she expected her to accept the penny story with much skepticism. But, as this was about her brother, Dorothy felt she should know about the appearance of the pennies.

The daughter listened patiently, but had no significant reaction.

A day later, Dorothy received a phone call from her daughter, who said she had something she needed to share with her mother. The daughter is a veterinarian. On the day after Dorothy called, she had completed an examination of an animal. She left the room to let the technician clean up prior to the next animal's visit. When the tech was done, she briefly stopped into the exam room to pick up a file. A penny was sitting on the steel exam table.

Dorothy's daughter went to the technician and asked why she had left a penny on the exam table. The technician said she had not left a penny on the table—that she never had money with her while she worked in the office. The room was totally clean when she had finished and the table was clear. The tech had no idea where the penny had come from.

Andrew's Dream

Nov. 1, 2003

My Dear Friend,

Last night was Halloween, and I was haunted not by ghosts and goblins, but memories of Alec. Last year for Halloween he had one of those memorable nights of youth. He and his dorm friends dressed up for the celebration. He wore a gorilla costume, and the kids tell us he had the time of his life. He hid behind trees and jumped out to scare other kids walking across campus, and there was a party at one of the frats. He was in total joy that night—savoring his young, emerging life at college. How much difference a year can make.

Today we went to JMU for Parents' Weekend. Our friends encouraged us to join them. We were there last year, of course, and this was a sort-of reunion. Ian was interested in going because he could spend the weekend with some friends there. And, we are encouraging him to seriously consider JMU. We knew it would be hard, but a good opportunity for Ian.

It was both painful and good—much like the rest of our lives right now. We went to see the kids at the apartment they are living in off campus—where Alec was supposed to live this year. It was odd—not really associated with him, but a place he was supposed to be, another step into his future. I was sorry that he was not there to enjoy it.

Andrew, Alec's good friend from high school, and

his roommate last year, told us about an extraordinary dream he had this past week. He dreamed he walked into his room at home, and Alec was there—just as he had always been, dressed in his typical jeans and T-shirt. He said Alec seemed to be aware that he had been away awhile, and began to ask Andrew how he was and what he'd been doing. Andrew anxiously asked Alec if he was OK. Alec assured that he was. Andrew asked about the accident, and what had happened, but Alec said the details were unimportant now.

Andrew asked him if there was a Heaven and what it was like. Alec told him there is a Heaven, but that Andrew was not to know the details of heaven until "his time." Alec told Andrew to hold onto his faith—that his faith would lead him to Heaven, and said that he, Alec, was where he needed to be, doing what he needed to do right now. Andrew asked what he was doing specifically. Alec replied that this was not something Andrew could know now, either. Then he asked Andrew to assure his friends that he was OK, that he was doing what was important to him.

Andrew told Alec that the others would want to see him, and that we would want to see him, but Alec said that for now, only Andrew would be able to do this. But he was to tell the others about him, and to emphasize that their faith was important.

Andrew said the dream was amazingly vivid, and that it has given him a great sense of peace. His girlfriend, Erica, also said that Andrew had found great comfort from it. It was important to him to tell us about it, and we were surprised to learn that he had not yet shared the dream with his parents.

He told us that it seemed totally real and so natural—just like when they lived together, and that he wished the conversation could have gone on late into the night, as it often did when they were roommates. He said the dream was different from most dreams—and, although logically he was tempted to dismiss it only as a dream, he felt like Alec had really come to him—to comfort him, and to comfort others by his sharing the experience. He also felt that Alec would eventually appear to others whom he loved to reassure them directly, as well.

Andrew is a young man who is faithful, but not terribly active religiously. Of Alec's friends, I would not consider Andrew one of the more fervent, nor one who typically talks about his beliefs and faith. Faith was a big thing for Alec, something he wrote a lot about in the past few years. It is interesting that this was a critical message that came from this dream.

I have felt all week that Alec's death is so unfair, truly monstrous. My emotions of resentment and anger seem to be growing as time moves on—so much we will miss with him, so little reason for this to have happened. But, tonight, I must say that Andrew's dream has brought some calm. Death seems so alien—I do not understand its relationship to our lives, particularly to young lives—but I know it comes to us all in "our time."

I feel that somehow my son knew and understood things in his short life that we have yet to know and understand. What was that, and why?

Eliza and Whitney's Party

June 8, 2004

The graduation events of 2004 were a bittersweet experience for so many of us. The class of 2004 (Ian's class) and the class of 2002 (Alec's class), shared friends from elementary school days, numerous siblings, and long-time dating relationships.

When the kids of 2004 graduated, the kids of 2002 were sure to be there to share in the experience and celebration. Coming just a year after Alec's death, there would be sadness along with the joy and anticipation of new beginnings.

Eliza and Whitney had a joint graduation party in Eliza's back yard. It was filled with old friends—families who have watched each other's kids grow up far too quickly.

All of the players were there, and one couldn't help but be happy for these accomplished young people as they reached this milestone in their lives. It was hard for us to be there without Alec—his friends surrounded us, and their presence made his absence more palpable.

Part way through the evening, JoRoyce walked over to sit with Bev and Ted. Both JoRoyce and Bev were silently thinking how wrong it was for Alec not to be at this event. As she sat down, JoRoyce looked down and saw a penny in the grass between her chair and Bev's. As always, we were somewhat disbelieving and amazed. We looked around—there were no other pennies on the ground to be found. It was impossible not to take it as a sign of Alec's presence.

In a few minutes, Tim came over to visit with us, and when he did, I said to him, "Tim, your buddy has been here." Tim was Alec's best friend. His parents had moved to another state and he had been living with us the summer Alec died. Our house was pleasantly filled with young men that June. For a few weeks we would enjoy a third son we had never had ourselves. Tim filled the guest room, but not as a guest. Understandably, he moved out the night Alec died. We not only lost Alec that summer, we also lost the summer with Tim.

He looked at me with confusion, and I reiterated, "Tim, Alec has been here—JoRoyce just found a penny on the ground between her and Bev." Tim seemed a bit confused, taken aback and uncomfortable with the comment, but replied politely, "I am sure he would want to be with us if he could, Mr. Robinson." And then, he quickly moved on to see some other friends.

It was unusual for me to make such a strong statement upon finding a penny in such a setting, and particularly to emphasize it to any of the kids. These experiences were hard for me to absorb, none-the-less for these young people. I scolded myself for being so blunt, and for disturbing Tim, but felt that the penny and its appearance between the moms was about as unquestionable a contact as it could be.

Then, I heard about Sharon's dream on June 10.

Sharon's Dream

On Friday, June 10, I ran down to Sharon and Doug's to borrow an egg—perhaps the first time ever. Tim and his dad were visiting, and I spontaneously decided to make strawberry shortcake, before checking ingredients in the house.

Sharon said she was glad I came down, for she had had a dream the night before about Alec, which was so memorable and so clear that she had not been able to get it out of her head.

Sharon and Doug went to the country to get a new dog. They arrived at a place with a long 3-board fence, against which were lined up all kinds of dogs—mostly Scotty dogs, all sizes and colors—all of them staring directly at Sharon.

As she looked at the dogs, she felt someone watching her. She turned around and Alec was standing behind her. In the dream she knew he had died, so she was surprised to see him there. She asked what he was doing there. He was dressed in his typical outfit of jeans, two layered shirts, sneakers, and wore a distinctive blue WWJD (What Would Jesus Do?) bracelet on his wrist.

Alec responded that he had come to talk with Sharon, to tell her about Heaven. He helped her off with her coat, and they went to sit in the back of a car. Sharon was excited, and asked what Heaven was like. He said it was indescribable. She said Alec had this extraordinary sense of peace and contentment. This was the strong, inescapable feeling she had in the dream and in the day afterward. She said he "glowed" with this sense of peace.

While in the car, one of Sharon's relatives came up to the window and yelled through it, "Sharon, what are you doing in there talking to yourself?" She realized that Alec was invisible to her relative.

Suddenly, JoRoyce and I drove up in our Toyota Highlander and parked right next to the car where Sharon and Alec sat. Sharon got out of the car and went to JoRoyce, saying, "Alec is sitting in the back of this car. He came to see me, but you are not going to be able to see him." Sharon could see Alec sitting in the car—his shoulder and his neck were visible through the open window, but he made no effort to look out to see JoRoyce. JoRoyce walked over to the window, stuck in her head, but could see no one.

At this point, the dream ended.

Sharon emphasized her sense that Alec was at peace and so totally content—that this was the meaning she drew from the dream. She felt the message was intentional. But, she said none of the rest of it made any sense to her. Did it to me?

To me, it all fit Alec so well—the Scotties and the Highlander represented his love for Scotland, and his strong pride in his Celtic heritage. He loved everything about that country. His outfit was his signature. Helping her off with her coat represented, for me, his courteousness and respect for Sharon. Sharon realized that the fence was the same as the fence at his accident site. The only piece that did not fit was the WWJD bracelet. Blue was his favorite color—that was significant—but the WWJD bracelet was not his style. He was very private about his religious beliefs. He would never have worn such a bracelet, especially so visibly.

I really questioned Sharon about this, and she said, "I am sure that's what he had on. It was just like the one Bill Thomas wears. He had one on the other night at Eliza's graduation party."

It took me until the next day to make the connection—Eliza's party was where the penny appeared between JoRoyce and Bev, and I made the point so emphatically to Tim that Alec had been there with us. The blue WWJD bracelet was the connecting clue.

To me the message was clear. He wanted us to know he *was* with us that evening. My emphasis to Tim was not accidental. Sharon's dream was consistent with mine and with Andrew's. Alec wanted us to know that he was at peace and content, and he wanted us to know, as I had asked of him, that he was in Heaven.

"Listen to your life," said Ray. "Listen to your life."

Charlotte

In April 2004, I made a group business trip to Charlotte, NC.

The day before I left, we received a book from Life-Net, the organ procurement agency, commemorating the 2003 organ and tissue donors. Alec's picture and a dedication were in the book. I sat for a long time that evening looking at him, and looking at all the others who had died, but who had given so much in their last hours. It was hard to imagine all the stories represented by all of those people, and the loss that was reflected in the families' memories.

As I pored through the book, I kept looking at two coins on the coffee table—a nickel and a penny. They had been there several days. I assumed they had been left there by Ian, and he just never picked them up. But, I couldn't help but think about all of the coins that had appeared over the past months. With the LifeNet book and the coins, it was hard not to recall a lot of memories about Alec. There I sat for the longest time, lost in my memories and thoughts about the events of the past year.

The next morning I left early for Charlotte. It was a short trip, so I had one small bag. When we arrived in Charlotte, we were immediately put on a bus to begin an orientation to the city. Our luggage was taken by separate vehicle directly to the hotel and would be waiting in our rooms when we checked in.

We finally got to our rooms about 6:00 P.M. I typically open the suitcase first thing—to hang shirts and dress clothes to allow the wrinkles to hang out. It was standing against the wall, and I put it on my bed to unpack. As I dug to the layer where my shirts were, I was stunned to find a nickel and a penny sitting perfectly on the top of my shirt stack. The suitcase had been packed up in our bedroom. The nickel and penny had been in the living room on a coffee table. I thought, just perhaps, I had unconsciously picked them up—but knew in reality there was no way.

I called JoRoyce that night and asked her if the nickel and penny were still on the coffee table. She went in to check, and they were still there. My suitcase had been in the luggage hold of the plane, on a van, transported to my room, moved from the floor to the bed. The probability of two coins sitting perfectly on top of my dress shirts was virtually impossible.

My thoughts of Alec and the coins had been inseparable the night before. Now I had the coins to remind me that he was never far away.

Butterflies in Colorado

During the summer of 2004, the Botanical Garden put on a major display of butterflies in its new conservatory.

Two groups of friends had contributed funds to the Garden in Alec's memory, and they wanted to make a gift of some permanent addition to the Garden.

We had found some stunning benches—steel cut into the shape of butterflies—which were perfect for the theme. And, the idea of metamorphosis—life reborn, life renewed, life in a new form—was also an apt theme for something to commemorate Alec's life. We asked that the gifts be used to purchase the butterfly benches, to be placed in front of the conservatory for the duration of the exhibit. They were a lovely aqua blue, and were striking in front of the shimmering glass building.

In June we took a short trip to Colorado. Ian's girl-friend's family had invited him to join them as a high school graduation gift. JoRoyce and I were also invited to join the family. We stayed in a lovely house near a mountain top, with spectacular views of the Breckenridge ski slopes. It was impossible to look at those mountains and not think of Alec—how he would have loved to be there, and how he would have been insistent that he would be back in the winter to snowboard. It had always been his dream to ski in the West. The very thought scared me—it seemed a formula for danger to let him snowboard down those long steep slopes of the Rockies. His eyes would have been afire with excitement. His cheeks would have glowed red in the fresh mountain air.

The second day in Breckenridge, we went to one of the ski slopes, which had bob sled-like rides down the mountain, and other amusements, for the summer season. JoRoyce and I decided to give it a go. We had a new camera, which we asked Linda and Dan to watch over while we rode down the mountain. After our runs down the hill, Dan said he had taken a few pictures. As we reviewed them, there was a gorgeous close-up of a pale blue butterfly sitting on some stones—unlike any of the "action shots" of the bobsledding. Linda said they had spotted it next to them, thought it was lovely, and just happened to get a perfect shot of it.

The next day, we stopped at a local diner for lunch in Frisco. One of the touches of local flavor was the use of small platters on which our lunches were served, all of which had been decorated and fired at a local kiln. Everyone at the table had a different design—geometric with abstract splashes of color, except for mine. My platter had a blue butterfly in the middle, with writing around the edge which read, "What the caterpillar sees as the end of life, the butterfly sees as a beginning of new life.."

I looked around the restaurant, and could find no other platter with writing around the rim. When we finished dining, I told the waitress that I had received the butterfly platter, and had noticed that no-one else seemed to have one just like it. I said I was curious if they used a lot of butterfly platters in the restaurant that perhaps I had not seen. She replied that almost all the platters were different, and I was just lucky enough to have gotten the butterfly for my lunch.

On our last day in Colorado, we rented bikes for the kids and needed to transport them to a starting place for their bike ride down the mountain. This necessitated folding down the seats of the cars we had rented. When I did, I found under the back seat, a single turquoise metallic butterfly—the kind you would put into a card, or sprinkle on a table for a party. There were a few small crumbs of a pretzel and the one butterfly under that seat. Nothing else—it was perfectly clean except for those two things.

In three days in Colorado, we experienced 3 blue butterflies. Three manifestations of wonder.

Jayson's Story

On the first anniversary of Alec's death, Jayson appeared at our door.

Jayson and Alec had been inseparable friends in middle school. They attended separate high schools, and different colleges, but the sense of closeness had remained between the two.

Jayson carried a baseball, a cap, and a card in hand. He was a pitcher on his college baseball team. After Alec died, Jayson decided to dedicate his sophomore year of baseball to Alec—to honor their friendship and recognize its importance in his life.

Jayson had a terrible year. He couldn't stay focused. He pitched badly. The team had a lousy standing. He felt like he had let everyone down, including Alec. Here he had committed the season to Alec, and it was the worst in his life.

Tournament time came around, and there were no high hopes for the team. Jayson certainly wasn't going to get to play much. But the lead pitchers on the team were both injured. Jayson took the mound. He pitched a perfect game, and his team won the tournament.

At the end of the game, his parents noticed that Jayson stayed in the dugout, and was in no hurry to join the other players, and that he seemed to be talking to someone. It was Alec. He said he realized that Alec had been with him all year, but he was trying to teach him an important lesson—to persevere, to never give up, and to have faith.

Jason had written Alec's initials on his cap at the beginning of the season. He wanted us to have it, along with the tournament game ball, in recognition of this presence he felt from Alec, and a friendship that continued beyond death.

Revelation at Tofuku-ji

October 26, 2005

Today I visited Tofuku-ji, one of the major Zen Buddhist temples in the southern part of Kyoto, founded in 1236.

As many times as I've been here, I have never been to Tofuku-ji, partly because it is off the beaten track, and partly because the gardens were re-created in 1939, and thus considered new, even though they were designed to reflect back to the simple styles and values of the Kamakura Period (12th and 13th centuries) when the temple was established. These were Confucian beliefs of simplicity, loyalty to family, high discipline and strong personal morals.

I went to see the gardens, which are best known for their stark geometric simplicity—rectangular stones set in a sea of moss in one area, azaleas sheared into perfect rectangular cubes in contrast with moss and stone in another part of the garden. These are symbolic of yin-yang, positive-negative unity, and supposed reference to ancient Chinese and Japanese land planning schemes.

What I was surprised to find were two little-referenced raked gravel Zen gardens, which I found to be quite different from others I have seen, and I found to be quite exciting. The southern garden is the largest, and is composed of rock clusters representing the Japanese Elysian Islands (Paradise) set in a sea of gravel representing the "eight rough seas." The second east garden is much smaller, and represents the Great Bear constellation, Ursa major, which we also know as the Big Dipper.

The southern garden immediately made me think of van Gogh's famous painting *Starry Night*. The gravel pattern is amazingly complex. I cannot imagine how one rakes this and successfully backs out of it with no footprints or trace left behind.

The images of van Gogh would not leave my head. When I got back to the room, I decided to look them up on the internet. I was amazed to find that the well known *Starry Night Over the Rhone* (1888) exactly illustrates Ursa major! In Greek mythology, this constellation is part of the gardens of the Hesperides—islands in the mystical west where grows a golden apple tree, which bears immortality-giving fruit. In fact, the three major stars of Ursa major are the apples themselves. The Hesperides were also known in ancient days as the Fortunate Islands, and Islands of the Blest (Celtic mythology).

The second van Gogh, *Starry Night,* (1889) is the one that is so similar to the raked gravel at Tofuku-ji. I looked it up at the Museum of Modern Art site, and found the following interpretation. "Van Gogh's night sky is a field of rolling energy. Below the exploding stars, the village is a place of quiet order. Connecting earth and sky is the flame like cypress, a tree traditionally associated with graveyards and mourning. But death was not ominous for van Gogh. 'Looking at the stars always makes me dream, he said. Why, I ask myself, shouldn't the shining dots of the sky be as accessible as the black dots on the map of France? Just as we take the train to get to Tarascon or Rouen, we take death to reach a star.'"

Interesting to consider death a transport, as opposed to thinking of it as an end, or even a new beginning. The Celts described it as a journey—traveling over "the river hard to see."

Those who knew Alec know how much he loved to look at the stars at night.

It seems no matter where I go I find links back to him, and reference to Paradise and eternity. On my way here, I read an article about Mormonism. One of its important tenets is God's ongoing revelation to us. I think they have this one right, if we keep our hearts and our minds open.

Pennies seem to be in short supply here, but as I made my way back to the hotel today, a Japanese paperclip mysteriously appeared in my pocket.

"Listen to your life," said Ray. "Listen to your life."

Part III

The Community

The Community

What do you do when someone loses a child?

We were blessed with support and caring in our community that was beyond our conception. We were surrounded immediately by so many family and friends.

I am most grateful for those who came to be with us—whose physical presence said all that was needed. They appeared like magic, in waves, day and night. I am sure I missed scores of them, but for every body that took the time to come to us, I am eternally grateful. As the reality hit, each hug, each kiss, each touch was a gift.

I recall the friends who met me at the airport, who greeted me with open arms as I departed from the arrival gate. It was that moment I knew this was not all a nightmare. Had it been a dream, they would not be there to greet me. As they embraced me my heart knew the truth, and it burst in pain.

I recall those standing in the yard as I arrived home—our friend Joy, whose house Alec loved to visit for its warmth and welcome. Joy was so aptly named—always full of kindness and smiles. She was crying in our yard. I had never seen her cry before.

I remember the throng in the house as I entered. Friends, neighbors and kids at every glance.

I was so stunned that someone mowed my grass, and someone else walked the dog routinely. People answered the phone, received the mail, responded to the door, brought us food and drink. Someone ran the vacuum at the end of the evening and straightened up the house.

I am thankful for the friend who called a physician who quietly watched us for hours, and then went to the pharmacy to get us some medication, which he insisted on paying for himself; for the friend who was a grief counselor who came and quietly talked with us; for the friend who came and asked if I would like to talk "about him," to tell him what Alec was like—it was such a joy to talk about his life!

Alec's college friends were so absolutely amazing. They were so strong, and so caring. They brought pictures to share, they sat on his bed and told us stories about him at college—things he never would have told us. These stories of his life were such gifts—little vignettes of him we never would have known. At that stage of my life I would have run from death. I would have not known what to say. These kids were so incredible—pillars of strength—such a reflection of my son!

Flowers and food poured in. The phone rang. People kept records of who brought and sent what, and who called. They screened the phone calls, and came to us when they thought we needed to talk to someone directly. Others called friends to be sure people knew about Alec's accident. The thoroughness of their efforts was indescribable. One friend suggested we set up a memorial fund in lieu of flowers, and then proceeded to call Alec's school to make those arrangements.

When the organ donation agency called, someone stood with me, holding on to my shoulders as I made those awful decisions. Could they take his ribs? . . . body part by body part . . . how does one survive alone after that conversation?

Our minister came to plan the funeral, and personally took us to the funeral home to select the casket, and to the cemeteries to find a plot. He drove us from place to place and gently guided us through each decision. We could barely think, nevertheless drive to and from these places.

We had calling hours at the funeral home and were overwhelmed with the outpouring of friends and co-workers. We found strength and hope with each individual word of kindness and each caress.

People filled the church to overflowing. We peeked from around the door stunned as the ushers put up more and more chairs. Every body, every face in that crowd was a gift—to know so many cared. So many traveled from so far away—some people we had not seen in years. The families of the church put on an indescribable reception after the memorial service. Friends at the church provided the flowers as a gift, and even went to our house to pick flowers from our garden to include in the pall.

Some friends negotiated room rates and made reservations for out-of-town family at a local hotel, and then picked up the tab before anyone could check out.

Cards came daily in the mail for more than a year. There are hundreds, maybe more than a thousand. I won't count them, for if there were a thousand more, I would be equally as grateful for each one—for the effort and outreach to a family in need. Some were profound. Others just said hello.

I remember one of Alec's high school teachers writing to say how much she would miss him, and that she would most miss his smile—Mrs. Ford knew the special nature of this child. Alec's friends wrote and sent photos from their personal collections just to be sure we had pictures which were special to them. One friend traveled through France for the summer and lit a candle for him in each cathedral she visited, and then sent us a picture of each of those churches.

I am so grateful to the neighbor whom we had never met who took the time to write a lovely note in a card. I am grateful for the friend of ten years who came to share that he and his wife had lost a child—we never knew—and of the care we needed to take of each other in the months and years ahead.

Alec's high school principal called to say that the photography company that did graduation pictures was sending a complete portfolio of the photographs they had of him as a gift to us. Such a treasure! Could they ever know what that meant to us? Every picture was precious now.

The President of his college, James Madison University, called personally to express his condolences. One of Alec's friends had called JMU to let them know he had died.

The kids from Ian's class signed huge scrolls of paper with greetings and encouraging words to our family. We keep them still.

Memorial gifts were sent to work, to his school, to

our church. They allowed us to focus on positive things we could do to honor his life and help others as he might.

Alec's photography teacher from high school, Mr. Martin, who was an especially inspiring teacher to Alec, sent images from his portfolio. They included his photo of the eternal flame from the Holocaust Museum in Paris.

One of the very early coincidences came the first time we decided to get out of the house. My sister Sandy was staying with us to help out, and we decided to go have some lunch in one's of Alec's favorite restaurants. After lunch we strolled a bit as she was unfamiliar with that area of town. I took her to my favorite furniture store and we were amazed to be staring at a magnificent photograph of Paris hanging directly across from the entry. All of the places we had visited and enjoyed so much as a family were in that photograph. The next day, I went back to buy it, and hung it over the mantle of our family room.

One of our good friends recognized it as new, and its significance to us. In just a day we received a card and credit notice—a group of our friends chipped in to buy the picture for us, and there was no charge to our account. The card simply said, "May your memories of Paris be happy ones."

In that first year, many people kindly invited us to their homes or out to events. We declined more than we accepted. Mourning is draining, and spouses each mourn on their own schedules. Some days one of us was ready to go and the other wasn't. Some days it just didn't feel right to celebrate or socialize. New people were awkward around us when they heard that our son had died. I remember being petrified about being asked the question, "How many children do you have?" I didn't have an answer I had peace with. So often, if we were with friends, conversation turned to the kids. We always cared about what others' kids were doing, but there was always this big shadow in the chatter.

It was important to be asked, however, and we were grateful for people's efforts to keep us involved. We had to take baby steps back into some sense of normalcy. The ongoing invitations made that possible. We always hoped those we said "no" to were understanding and patient.

One time we did say "yes." A very generous family offered us their weekend house in the mountains. It was winter, and getting away for a couple of days seemed OK. In all honesty, in those first months we were afraid to be away—alone with our thoughts and time on our hands sounded less like relaxation and more like torture. It is hard to control what comes to one's mind when there is unstructured time. Ian invited his best friend, Justin, to join us, and in turn, each boy brought his girlfriend. With four teenagers in the car and in the house, for the first time in months it felt like we were an intact family again. The void of Alec's absence did not disappear, but it was buffered by those four young, expansive spirits as they explored the house, chose bedrooms, stayed up late in front of the fire talking and giggling. As we lay in bed listening to them, it seemed like life could be normal again—some day. One never knows where he might find some peace and comfort. This weekend, i was in the mountains.

Another unexpected gift came from a long-time friend who lives at quite a distance. She heard a program on National Public Radio and subsequently purchased a CD and mailed it to me. It was a work by John Rutter, an internationally known British composer of choral music. The composition was entitled *Mass of the Children*.

John Rutter had a musically talented son who was a member of the choir at Clare College, Cambridge, John Rutter's alma mater. As I understand the story, Christopher Rutter, 19, was struck by a car and killed in front of the chapel as he was leaving choir practice one evening in March 2001. His father was unable to compose music for nearly two years, but when he began again, he wrote *Mass of the Children*. It is an exquisite piece.

Music had become absent from my life, even though it has been intrinsic to it from the time I was a child. It became too painful—too close to the hole in my heart after Alec died. Somehow, with the similarities of our losses—sons 19 inexplicably struck down at the prime of their lives—I felt perhaps this was a window. If Rutter could compose, knowing his broken heart, I could listen. Through it—its glorious voices and magnificent movements—music has entered my life again. Not in full measure, but to a degree. The last movement ends with "Dona nobis pacem"—give us peace. Is this not, ultimately, what we all ask of God?

My intent is to emphasize that there are so many opportunities to provide support. Each interaction, (no matter how insignificant it may seem to the outsider), to a family in crisis, is a big thing, with long impact and appreciation. To those who do not know what to say, say nothing, but do something.

We live in a community which seems to have an unusual capacity for support and organized response, and we are blessed to have such loyal and caring friends. But, there is no reason every town can't be like ours.

Even now, more than two years after Alec died, we run into people who say, "I heard about your son, and I am so sorry. I meant to call or drop a line, but I just did not know what to do or say. I did not want to make you remember, or make you sad."

We understand—there are no adequate words, and little prepares any of us for such a difficult situation. But in truth, any gesture speaks loudly—and there is no way we can ever forget, and there is nothing anyone can say that could make us any sadder than we already are.

When Your Child Dies

When your child dies you immediately fall into the deep shaft of a well.

There is no day or night. There is barely enough air to breath. The world around you is a cacophony of noise and confusion.

Your world closes in. Unexpectedly and uncontrollably you find yourself in the middle of an insanity, an unbelievable reality, which you pray will go away with the next second—if you can only wake up. If you sleep, you dream nightmares. When you wake, you immediately think, "My God, Alec is dead."

You are out of control of your life. You have been abandoned. You have been violated in the most cruel and unfair way by life, and by God himself.

You must do things you should never do—would never want to do—select a coffin, plan a funeral service, choose burial clothes. One minute you were normal, the next minute your life is shattered. You are worried about the welfare of your spouse, your children, your parents—how will they survive this?

You forget to eat. You cannot sleep. You are both numb and absolutely raw. You are confused and overwhelmed—you know this cannot be real. Time slows down, but there is a tornado of activity surrounding you. You hate this. You want it all to go away. You know there has been a mistake. How could so many people be wrong?

Your child is dead.

You feel utterly and absolutely alone.

Psalm 23

I have never understood the comforts of the 23rd Psalm and its ubiquitous reading at Christian funerals.

Its shifting images and metaphors confuse and jar me more than ensure me of the Lord's guidance and comfort.

Don't we walk through the true "valley of death" versus the "valley of the shadow of death"? The shadow of death may create anxiety in us, but the real "death valley" is what breaks us—the antithesis to human life. It is when I am in the valley of death that I want to "fear no evil."

Yet, there has been, through this grief, an insight into the intent of this psalmist.

"He restoreth my soul."

If there is any one truth to my experience as a grieving father—after months of immeasurable kindness, time, company, comforting, food, letters, cards, phone calls, shared tears, and quiet mutual silence—one day, upon the receipt of a gift from a friend, I understood. "He restoreth my soul." Judy's gift tipped the scales, and for the first time, I could see.

He has restored my soul through love and generosity; love that has filtered through a thousand hands and hearts; love that has arrived in the most ordinary and extraordinary ways; love that appears to be inexhaustible.

God has not mended my broken heart. He has not answered the question I have asked Him for the millionth time. He has not performed the miracle which I have asked of Him almost every day. And, He has not granted me my wish to join my son—to be at his side to father him, love him and care for him, as I know I am supposed to do.

But, He has restored my soul, speck by tiny speck, minute by tiny minute, grace by tiny grace.

And, perhaps that is all I can ask.

Kathy's Gift

On the night of Alec's accident a young woman named Kathy Robinson was routinely driving home and came upon the accident scene. She was the first to arrive, who called the rescue squad, who turned off the car engine. With time, others arrived, and Kathy ferociously protected the car and Alec, not allowing anyone to come near until the EMS took control. No-one quite understood.

Kathy came to the funeral home and the funeral. We saw her a couple of times when we were at the accident site, as she lived on the same road. But, we have never shared much conversation with her. It was too hard to even imagine what we might discuss.

Just before the first anniversary of Alec's death, we received the following letter from Kathy. In a few simple lines, she turned a moment of horror, a moment which we could barely consider, into something holy.

Kathy's gift.

May 3, '04

Dear Frank,

I truly understand your great loss in your life. Because I didn't know Alec at all but since that night God showed me that life is to (sic) short and by me being with Alec that night that he had passed away he went peaceful.

His body changed colors in front of my face and I saw his spirit leave (h)is body. And what I saw that night I didn't let know (sic) one around his car because what happen (sic) within the car that night I knew God had stepped in and was taking control of the matter. He sent his angels down to Alec to take him home. And they did when the rescue squad people came to the seen (sic) of the accident they told me to set in my car I did what they said to do. One of them came to my car and told me that he didn't make it. I said you don't have to tell me I already know. But, he is alright he is gone on home to be with his savior Jesus Christ. When they covered the car tears rolled down my face. I felt like someone had pulled my heart out of my chest. I felt like I had known Alec for a long time. Since that night I go that way all the time. When I feel sad or depressed I go there it helps me a lot. I pick the site up all the time. I also leave gifts there for him because I feel that he is a part of my life. I put the red cardinal out there. For Easter I put a Easter basket out there. Some red, orange + yellow flowers and a windmill with a angel on it. Alec had made a big difference in my life and my Family. I have been going to church all that I can. I take Alec's picture with me all the time. It gives me peace of mind. I know one day when I am going that way I am going to see him again deep within my hearts and soul I am ready and looking forward to see him. Because right now there is something that I don't know or understand but maybe its (sic) not for me to understand at this moment or this day in time but God knows the reason and purpose. Someday when you and your family is ready to visit I will be here.

Until we see you again,
please take care,
and God Bless
you and your Family.

With love,
Kathy

Notes

1. *Emmanuel's Book*, compiled by Pat Rodegast and Judith Stanton. Copyright 1985. Used by permission of Random House, Inc.

2. *Dog Song*, a story by Ann Pancake. Copyright 2004. Used by permission of the author.

3. *West Side Story*, "I Have a Love." Used by permission of Universal Music Publishing Company.

4. "Briefly It Enters, and Briefly Speaks" by Jane Kenyon. Copyright 2005 by the Estate of Jane Kenyon. Reprinted from *Collected Poems*, with the permission of Graywolf Press, Saint Paul, MN.

5. Reprinted with the permission of Scribner, an imprint of Simon and Schuster Adult Publishing Group, from *I and Thou* by Martin Buber, translated by Walter Kaufmann. Copyright 1970 by Charles Scribner's Sons.

6. *A Grief Observed* by C.S. Lewis, copyright C.S. Lewis Pte. Ltd. 1961. Used by permission.

7. *Rinkitink in Oz* by L. Frank Baum. Used by permission of Dover Publications.

8. "When You Come Back Down," by Danny O'Keefe and Tim O'Brien. Copyright 1997. Used by permission of the composers, Mighty Nice Music, Bicameral Songs, and Howdy Skies Music.

9. "Can't Keep" by Eddie Vedder. Lyrics reprinted courtesy of Innocent Bystander. Copyright 2002. All rights reserved.

A Note on the Type

The text of *Alec's Legacy* has been typeset in **Galliard**, a font that was once the name of a type size (9 point), as well as a dance and its musical form. The family of type now known by this name was designed by Matthew Carter. It is based on the designs of the sixteenth-century French typecutter Robert Granjon, one of the finest punchcutters who ever lived. Galliard is Carter's homage to the man as well as to his work.

The font used for the book title and display titles in the text is **Colmcille**, designed in the mid-1930s by Colm O'Lochlainn, a Gaelic scholar, typographer, and printer. O'Lochlainn named the font to honor the 6th Century saint, Colmcille (also known as St. Columba), a leader of the early Celtic church in Ireland and Scotland. Colmcille was a renowned scribe who trained his monks to become master scribes. Colmcille's monks ultimately created the exquisite Irish masterpiece, the *Book of Kells*. Colmcille also founded the famous Christian monastery on the Isle of Iona, Scotland.